DIY DYE

Published in the U.S. by
Ulysses Press
P.O. Box 3440
Berkeley, CA 94703
www.ulyssespress.com

ISBN: 978-1-64604-264-7
Library of Congress Control Number 2013947585

Printed in the United States

10 9 8 7 6 5 4 3 2 1

Acquisitions Editor: Katherine Furman
Editor: Melanie Gold
Proofreader: Mary Hern
Design and layout: Ashley Prine
Indexer: Jay Kreider, J S Editorial

Cover photographs: yellow hair © vita khorzhevska/shutterstock.com; pink hair © Aleksandar Bozhikov/shutterstock.com; green hair © Aleksandar Bozhikov/shutterstock.com; purple hair © Tawin Mukdharakosa/shutterstock.com; red hair © Subbotina Anna/shutterstock.com; orange tube dye © r3rn/shutterstock.com; chalk © tuchkay/shutterstock.com; purple brush © Jason Hofmann/shutterstock.com.

Interior photographs: © Jason Hofmann except pages 4–5, 30–31 © veralub/shutterstock.com; pages 16–17 © Eldad Carin/shutterstock.com; pages 24–25 © Danylo Staroshchuk/shutterstock.com; page 37 © haveseen/shutterstock.com; pages 38–39 © RLN/shutterstock.com; pages 44–45 © art_of_sun/shutterstock.com; pages 54–55 © oriontrail/shutterstock.com; pages 60–61 © Subbotina Anna/shutterstock.com; page 67 © GVictoria/shutterstock.com; page 77 lemon © Chrstian Jung/shutterstock.com, chamomile © Picsfive/shutterstock.com, and cinnamon © B. and E. Dudzinscy/shutterstock.com.

DIY DYE

BRIGHT AND FUNKY TEMPORARY HAIR COLORING YOU DO AT HOME

LOREN LANKFORD

PHOTOGRAPHY BY JASON HOFMANN

ULYSSES PRESS

CONTENTS

INTRODUCTION 7

GET READY 9
MATERIALS.......................... 10
COLOR WHEEL—BASE COLOR 10
THE BLEACH SPEECH 12
A WORD OF CAUTION 13
WHAT TO EXPECT
WHEN YOU'RE DYEING.................... 13

THE DYES....................... 15
BLEACH RECIPE
AND TECHNIQUES 17
HAIR CHALKING
RECIPES AND TECHNIQUES 25
KOOL-AID RECIPE
AND TECHNIQUES 31
COLORED-HAIRSPRAY
TECHNIQUES.........................39
HENNA RECIPES
AND TECHNIQUES 45

FOOD-COLORING
RECIPES AND TECHNIQUES 55
STORE-BOUGHT
COLORING TECHNIQUES 61

DIY STYLE....................... 69

FULL HEAD............................ 70
STREAKS, HIGHLIGHTS,
AND LOWLIGHTS 73
OMBRE 78
JUST THE TIPS 82
TWO-TONE 85
RAINBOW 89

INDEX...94

ABOUT THE CONTRIBUTORS 96

ACKNOWLEDGMENTS 96

INTRODUCTION

It's crazy to think that there are people in this world (tons of them!) who have "virgin hair," meaning they've never used dye. There are also tons of people who only use dye to enhance the shade they naturally have. Many of these gals and guys were born with "dishwater blond" or "mousy brunette" hair and get highlights or lowlights or some mix of the two in order to take things up a notch. And then there's me.

If you can find the shade on a color wheel, my hair has been there. Throughout middle school and high school my hair was every color from green to pink to highlighter yellow to purple to black and every combination in between. I used Manic Panic hair paint and was actually thrilled to find out that the chlorine in the pool where I worked would turn my hair the fiercest shade of puke green (forgive me, hair gods! I knew not what I wrought).

I did it because choosing to dye your hair—and in what ways—says a lot about your personality and the kind of image of yourself you want to project to the world. Much like your fashion choices or preferred makeup style describe *you* to those around you, your hair color and the way it is laid out might say that you're a fiery redhead at heart or a wannabe blonde.

You don't have to be quite as experimental as my sixteen-year-old self in order to dabble with dyeing your hair. No matter where you fall along the spectrum and whether you dye at home or at a salon, there are hundreds of different ways to enhance your look. Worried about screwing up? Try to remember that it's just hair—you can redo it or a stylist can work magic on it, and if nothing else, it'll grow back! If I could attend my first movie premiere with (accidental) gray hair, you can overcome your mistakes as well.

GET READY

BEFORE YOU START CANDY-COATING
YOUR LOCKS, THERE ARE A FEW THINGS
YOU NEED TO KNOW.

MATERIALS

Obviously there are different materials you will need for each specific type of dye and style, but here are the things you'll need on hand no matter how you choose to dye:

- Painting clothes, like an old T-shirt and pants (to wear while you dye)
- Rubber gloves
- Hairbrush or comb

COLOR WHEEL—BASE COLOR

If you have blond or light hair, you've basically hit the hair-dye jackpot. Any color that you want to use (purple, red, black, etc.) will dye well right onto your current palette after using a toner. That's the key. The lighter your hair color is after using a toner, the more vibrant the color will show up. Dyeing right on top of gray hair will also get you super-vibrant results.

Think of it like this: You have a piece of white paper and crayons. When you draw red on the paper, it comes up . . . well, really red! But if you then take a brown piece of construction paper and put it on the red, you're not just going to get brown—you're going to get a marriage of the two! So, depending on the color you want, you must consider your current color and how the two will mix. That's why it's important to remember the color wheel you learned as a kid in art class. If you're trying to go bright red and you put that over yellow, your hair will be orange. If you put blue on yellow, your hair will turn green.

If you're a brunette and you want to dye your hair purple, using purple dye directly on your brunette hair will show up as burgundy and might not have quite the effect you want (unless what you want is a faint, darker tone). For color that is vibrant and lasting, bleach your hair first.

The same goes for those of you who have super-dark hair. You're going to have to do the most work to get a really bright shade of any funky colors like red, purple, pink, or green. You will need to use bleach, not high lift color, and in doing so run the risk of damaging your hair, so use a protein treatment

beforehand. If you're feeling a little nervous about going blonde on your own, you may want to have a professional get you there so you have a nice blank canvas to put some bright colors on.

An alternative for dyeing dark hair is to use a color treatment that sits on top of your natural color. Chalks and colored hairsprays don't actually dye your hair. Instead they coat it and will show up beautifully on any color of locks. The only downside (or upside, depending on what you're looking for) is that the color will come out in one wash. The upside is you can color-coordinate to your outfits every day! Much more on these later.

High lift tint works a lot like bleach, without all the added drying out and stripping of the hair. Which probably leaves you thinking, *If it's better, why don't people use it as often?* Well, it's not nearly as strong and is usually only used on virgin hair. Categorized as a level ten or higher, high lift tint can help you become the lightest version of the color you already have. If it'll work for you, use it! It also works as a toner, which can help eliminate one step of the process. Blondes and light brunettes, give it a try, especially if you want highlights or lowlights. Everyone else, it's bleach for you, my friend. Remember that bleach only removes color, it doesn't add anything in. High lift, often seen in boxed colors, works with what you've got.

THE BLEACH SPEECH

The darker your hair, the longer the bleach will need to stay on, and you'll want to keep a watchful eye on it. Once your hair is coated in bleach, it will take from ten minutes to half an hour, depending on how dark your hair is and how light you want to go, for you to reach platinum blond. You'll notice your hair turning orange, but don't freak out and wash it out! Leave it in and it will continue to bleach lighter. For jet-black hair, you may need to bleach twice to achieve the effect you want. If you do find yourself needing to bleach twice or rebleach, it's best to wait approximately thirty-six hours between bleachings.

If you do make the bleach leap, be sure to wait at least a week after going to the light side before you throw the purple on top. Hair *is* fairly delicate, and you want to try to keep it healthy, especially if you plan to continue experimenting with dye in the future. (See pages 19–23 for instructions on using bleach with caution.)

Of course, when using something as strong as bleach, you always run the risk that the end result will come out too orange-y or yellowish no matter what you do. If this happens, your best bet is to deep-condition and use a semi-permanent color in a red tone. The red will take the orange to mahogany.

Remember that previously dyed hair and virgin hair will usually show slightly different results with regard to the vibrancy of the shade. It's also good to note that things like skin tone and eye color affect the overall look of hair color. When you look at a photo of a model and think, *Oh! I want her hair!*, simply buying the same shade doesn't guarantee it'll come out looking the same for you.

A WORD OF CAUTION

It's important to wear clothes and use towels that you don't mind getting dye on. It's best to work with your hair in the bathroom and cover the area with old towels or sheets in case of splattering. You should also immediately clean up your workspace, so than any errant dye is wiped up right away, when it's more likely to come off your counter, bathtub, or sink. Use bleach where needed. Likewise, if you accidently get dye on your forehead or earlobes while you work, it's best to tend to it right away while it's fresh. For the first few nights after you dye, it's also a good idea to place a towel over your pillowcase. Your hair will likely "bleed" until you've washed it a few times.

WHAT TO EXPECT WHEN YOU'RE DYEING

Different colors have different life expectancies, tendencies, and quirks. Here are tips on what you might get from some of the major hues.

RED / PINK

Note that pink hair color fades fast—even faster than red, which fades to pink pretty fast. You can keep pink in longer by not shampooing your hair very often and mixing some Manic Panic into your conditioner when you do wash. Without doing either of these, your pink will quickly fade to a pastel and then totally disappear within a few weeks. If you want to keep it around long term, you'll have to keep on dyeing!

BLUE / PURPLE

Like with many "loud" colors, one of the smartest things you can do to keep blue or purple going is shampooing your hair less often. You can also try to stick to only conditioning your tips, unless your hair just gets super oily (in which case feel free to condition all over every 3 days). It also helps to use a color-refreshing shampoo a few times a week, especially if you have particularly dry hair.

GREEN

Again, you'll want to wash your hair less often and try to use the coldest water possible. For a unique green color, you can try mixing different shades of green or adding in some blue to the mix. Avoid highly chlorinated pools or high sun exposure, as this will drain the color. To keep your color up, touch up any problematic or light areas every 2–4 weeks.

YELLOW / ORANGE

So, you want your hair the color most people who spend their time trying to go blonde totally dread. You'll dye the same way you do blonde, bleaching until white and then dyeing on top of that. However, you can worry less if you have trouble getting totally blonde. Skip the toner and conditioners at first and just dye on however blonde you can get, and then once your dye has set, you can always tone to sharpen the color if you aren't happy.

THE DYES

FROM HOME-GROWN TO STORE-BOUGHT,
HERE ARE ALL THE BEST CONCOCTIONS
TO GET HAIR "TO DYE FOR."

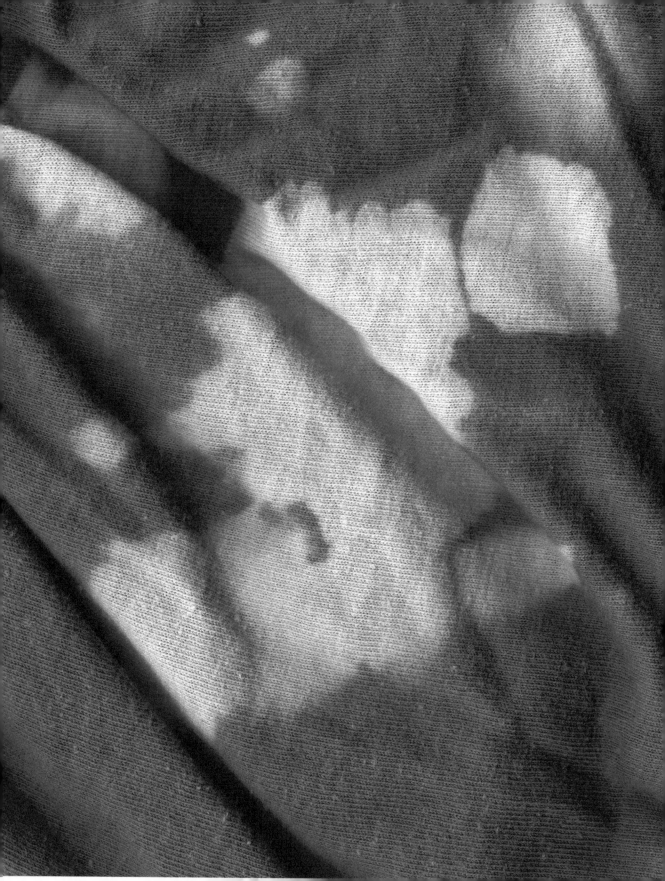

BLEACH RECIPE AND TECHNIQUES

Since bleaching may be the first step toward your ultimate new hue, let's talk about it first. Bleaching your hair is among the most intense things you can do to your mane. It's easy to mess it up, and the components are often harsh and can cause your hair to become super-brittle or damaged. While bleaching is a common practice at salons and among professional hair stylists, bleaching at home requires thorough research and a solid skill set to pull off correctly.

While many DIY hair gurus would go ahead and just advise you to head to a salon to go blond *before* attempting something on top of your new white 'do, I want to show you healthy-haired ladies the safest way out there to achieve the look you're going for at home. Since so many colors pop better with a blond base (red, pink, and blue come to mind), it's no wonder it's a popular technique to try out.

To go the home route, you'll need a professional-grade bottle of bleach and developer. I recommend going with a 30, as using anything higher can lead to major mistakes. You don't want to dye your hair only to find it falling out afterward! Scary, but it happens. I'd also recommend not skimping on the brands here. You're already saving money by doing it yourself, so wait until you have the cash (about $50, normally) to get some good stuff. Ask your local beauty-store employee what the best-selling bleaches and developers are, and read the boxes in-store, before purchasing. You may want to read some reviews online before you go to the store.

Developer is the ingredient that oxidizes your hair color and makes it stick to your hair permanently. It's the hair dye glue, basically. It works by opening the cuticle layer of the hair and allowing the color molecules to penetrate and color to be deposited into the cortex.

Developer comes in four volumes: 10, 20, 30, and 40. A 10-volume peroxide is the standard oxidizing strength for permanent, no-lift hair color. It's for when you just want to add a tint or color tone to hair of the same lightness level. Then 20 does the same thing but also lifts the hair's color level by 1–2 levels. This works well if you want to go one shade lighter than you already are. Next up is 30—the most common developer—which lifts you 2–3 levels and is used by those trying to go two shades lighter, or more. Finally, 40 should only be used in salons and by professionals.

I do want to state though, for the record, that if you have "tricky hair"—permed, heavily color-treated, super-curly, long, damaged, frizzy, very dark, etc.—it probably *is* better to have your hair double processed at a salon the first time you go blond, especially if you want to attain that elusive ice blond. Save those pennies, because someone who knows what they're doing shouldn't come cheaply for this overhaul. Once you're there and getting it done, you can talk to the stylist about the best ways to prolong your shade at home and save your dollars in the long run.

Double process is exactly what it sounds like: a coloring technique that requires two steps. It is sometimes referred to as "two-step coloring." Usually, the first step of this process is lightening. The second part is depositing the new color (if you're doing a color on your new blond) or toner (if you're keeping your new blonde shade). It can also mean coloring your hair one color and then adding highlights or lowlights.

MATERIALS

- Old T-shirt and towels
- Rubber gloves
- 1 packet of hair bleach
- Disposable mixing bowl
- Tint brush
- 30-volume developer
- Shampoo
- Conditioner
- Leave-in conditioner

The best way to prep—especially if you're starting with a dark base—is to treat your hair with leave-in conditioner a few weeks before you plan to dye. It's especially important to leave your ends saturated. You can also deep condition your hair in the shower about once a week. This way, your hair is in its most healthy state going into your transformation.

Once you've planned which day to dye, stop washing your hair. The longer you can go the better, but definitely don't wash your hair for at least three days before.

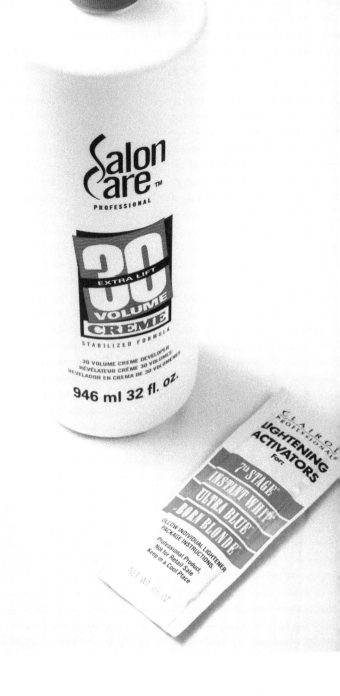

GET CRACKING

1. Bleach is strong! **Prep your space** for the bleaching process by laying down an old towel over any workspace you don't want to stain. Put on an old T-shirt, drape another old towel on your shoulders, and put on your rubber gloves.

2. Be sure to **follow the instructions** on your bleach and developer for mixing the two together.

TIPS TO DYE FOR
BLEACHING
A BIG MANE

Have a lot of hair to work with? Consider applying the bleach to your roots last. The roots will develop the fastest because of the heat from your scalp, and you don't want bleach sitting on them while you go around your whole head!

3 If you're doing your whole head, **divide your hair** into workable sections. Four will be good for short hair, but using six or more on longer hair will be helpful.

4 Take one section at a time and **paint the front and back of the hair strands, from the root down** to the very ends, saturating each section. It's more time consuming than just slopping it all on, but it's worth it!

5 Once you've covered everything you want, wait the amount of time suggested on your developer, though I wouldn't suggest going even a minute over one hour. A lot of times with hair dye, you can try to keep your hair saturated for ages before washing it out in hopes of really getting the color to stick. You don't want to do that here! Additionally, while your head will burn a little, **if you feel like your scalp is on fire, wash the stuff out immediately**. It's not worth damaging your hair or scalp! The right hairstylist can fix or advise on any horror-story hair situation, though I can't promise they won't slap your wrist for frying your locks!

6 During your wait-a-thon, you can check on your strands and watch them lighten or "lift." **Don't freak out if the color isn't exactly the color you wanted.** It's normal for the shade to be a bit off (and yellow-y, sometimes called "brassy") pre-toner. If your hair is orange and remains orange even after the full hour, wash everything out right away and either head to a salon or try again in a week. Might I suggest wearing an adorable beanie in the meantime?

7 Finally, you're ready to **immediately shampoo and condition** your hair. After that, you'll also want to apply the leave-in conditioner according to the instructions on the container. Your strands need all the nutrients!

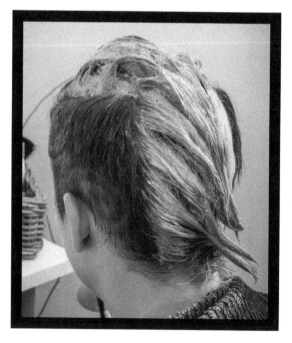

You might be happy with your results right off the bat—congrats, you're done! Or you may not yet have reached the shade you were going for. In that case, you can repeat the process. However, you should wait at least three days to do this and you shouldn't wash your hair during that wait time.

Once you've got the look you're going for, you can use a toner to even out the shine and shade. I love Manic Panic's Virgin Snow, but you should research what color you're looking for and use what's best for you and your hair.

If blonde was what you were after, congrats, you're done! Shampoo your hair daily with a blond-specific shampoo and conditioner. You can retone if any discoloration happens (hello, creeping yellow-y hue), but if you were going blond only as a base color, you're now ready to apply color.

TIPS TO DYE FOR
WANNA GO WILD?

If your style is to keep very short hair that gets buzzed with a clip down to about a half-inch or so, you can have a lot of fun bleaching patterns into your hair. All you need to do is cut out whatever shapes you like from some thin cardboard, like an old cereal box. You can do stars, polka dots, or even some leopard print.

Hold the cardboard stencil against your hair until the hair pokes through the shapes you cut. Then paint the bleach on and remove the cardboard. Rinse after the allotted time and you're done!

Didn't turn out like you hoped?

Shave it off!

HAIR CHALKING RECIPE AND TECHNIQUES

Of all of the temporary ways to dye your hair, hair chalk is the best option for those who want to experiment without much of a commitment. Because it's super-trendy right now, there are tons of hair chalks on the market in every color imaginable that you can easily apply for a one-day use and wash out. Most of the hair chalks out there are very similar to art pastels used for drawing, and a lot of people just use those because they're so easy to find. But if you love DIY and want to make your own custom colors that work best for your hair, you'll probably prefer to make your own.

The brightness of the shade will of course depend on your starting color, but even those with dark hair can achieve a tinting effect with hair chalk. It's easy to apply and very easy to control, making it a perfect choice for someone who wants to apply a color only to their tips or as highlights but doesn't want to fuss with the messiness of actual hair dye.

You can buy chalk that is specifically made for your hair, or you can use regular soft pastels found in any art supply store.

First you have to decide where to chalk. If it's your first time out, you may want to begin by just doing your ends or one chunk of hair near the front of your face. Once you're used to the process, you can get more creative with how you apply it. One of my favorite looks is pulling half your hair back and just doing the hair underneath to achieve a peekaboo effect.

- Old T-shirt and towels
- Rubber gloves
- Chalk
- Spray bottle filled with water
- Flat iron or curling iron
- Hairspray

LOOK WHO'S CHALKING!

1. Begin by **prepping yourself for application**. Cover your workspace and your shoulders with a towel, or wear an old T-shirt that you won't mind staining. Put on gloves to protect your hands.

2. Using the spray bottle with water, **wet the part of your hair that you'd like to chalk**. If you're doing multiple areas (or all of your tips), start with one section at a time. You want to really saturate the hair without leaving it dripping wet.

3. Support the piece of hair you want to chalk in your palm. Hold the hair away from your head and, with your other hand, drag the chalk along the hair where you'd like the color to appear. **You'll want to really rub the chalk in**, going up and down and putting pressure against your other hand. No need to hurt yourself, but really get it in there! Move slowly to avoid crunching up your hair as you move up and down.

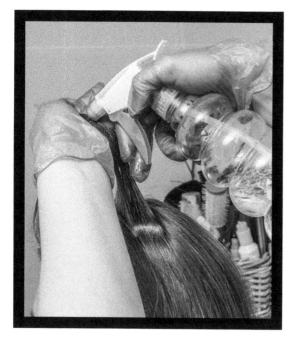
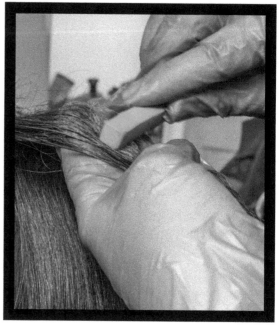

4 Once you feel like the color is pretty saturated on the strands, it's gonna look pretty chunky. Use a comb to **brush through the hair from top to bottom** to help evenly distribute the color.

5 **Repeat** this for each portion of hair you want to chalk.

6 Now, you'll want to **set the color by using heat**. You can either use a blow dryer and then a flat iron, or vice versa. (Note that using a straightener on wet hair is not the best idea for anyone with particularly sensitive or previously color-treated hair.) You can also wait for your hair to dry naturally, if you're patient.

7 Once you've dried and straightened all of the colored sections, use **hairspray on the colored** areas to prevent flaking.

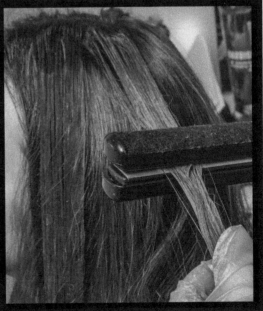

Voilà! Chalk will wash out in one to three shampoos. Those with light-colored hair will need more washes than those with dark-colored hair.

DIY HAIR CHALK

While it's probably easier to find hair chalk or soft pastels, sometimes it's really gratifying to build something from the ground up. If you're into doing things yourself, try out this chalk recipe.

MATERIALS

Disposable mixing bowl
½ teaspoon kaolin clay
2 tablespoons powder colorant in color of your choice
Small disposable microwavable mixing bowl
1 teaspoon arrowroot powder
½ teaspoon water
1 tablespoon witch hazel

MAKING HAIR CHALK

1 Mix the kaolin clay and powder colorant in a mixing bowl with your hands. (I like Bramble Berry neon pigments best, but any oxide pigment will work.)

2 In a smaller bowl, mix the arrowroot powder and water together.

3 Microwave the smaller bowl for three seconds in order to thicken the powder and water into a paste.

4 Using gloves, add witch hazel to the clay mixture and combine well.

5 Add the arrowroot mixture to the clay mixture and combine with your hands until you get a clay-like consistency. If it's too crumbly, try adding tiny amounts of witch hazel until you get the right consistency.

6 Shape the mixture to resemble a stick of chalk and lay it out to dry overnight (for about 12 hours).

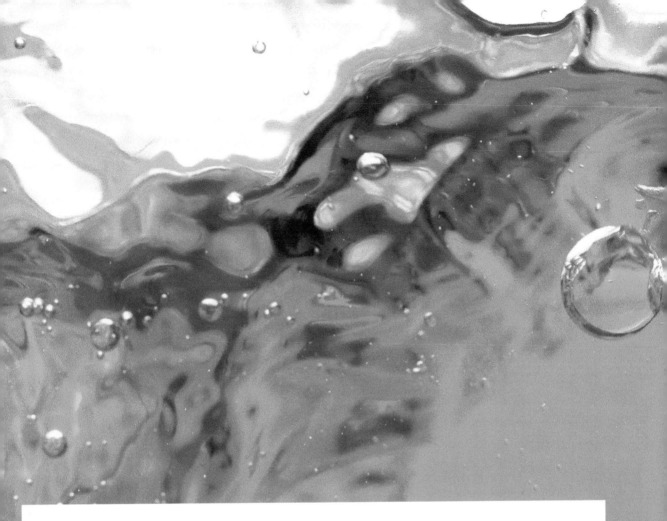

KOOL-AID RECIPE AND TECHNIQUES

When you're low on cash or just looking to experiment with something radically different on your hair (or all three things!), Kool-Aid is a fun new method to try out. Like any other form of hair coloring, different base colors mixed with different flavor-colors will produce different results. If you're feeling unsure of anything, you should try out one small section of your hair first before going whole hog.

Scared of commitment? Most of the time, Kool-Aid-dyed hair will wash out within two weeks. Of course, there is no hard line for anything, and the more color-treated, porous, and damaged your hair is, the more likely the color will stick it out longer. Red is the strongest color and most apt to hang around. It's also the most popular of the Kool-Aid treatments, and you can find tons of photos online for inspiration as you experiment.

MATERIALS

- Old T-shirt and towels
- Rubber gloves
- Vaseline
- 2 to 6 packets of unsweetened Kool-Aid (more if you have lots of hair and/or want a super-bright/vibrant color)
- Small bowl for each color
- 1 cup boiling water (but you won't need it all)
- Conditioner (optional)
- Tint brush
- Tin foil
- Plastic wrap or shower cap
- Old pillowcase
- Comb or brush

❋TIPS TO DYE FOR❋
KOOL HINTS

Prepare to dye at night!

Make sure you don't have sweetened Kool-Aid. It will make your hair sticky and could even irritate your skin and eyes.

This stuff can stain like crazy, so you really, REALLY need gloves and a covered work surface.

READY TO BE KOOL?
OHHHH YEEEEEEEAAH!

1. **Prep your space by** laying down an old towel over any workspace you don't want to stain. Put on an old T-shirt.

2. Decide **how many packets** you need. If you're doing your whole head and have a lot of hair, you might need five or six packets. Shorter hair? Thinner hair? Want to only do half of your hair? Figure on at least two packets, depending on your situation. Use your best judgment!

3 Put each **color powder into its own small bowl**.

4 Bring water to a **boil**.

5 BE SO SUPER CAREFUL!! as you add a ¼ **teaspoon of boiling water** into the bowl(s) and mix. Keep adding water until you get a thick paste with absolutely no lumps.

6 You can also **add conditioner if you want** a softer color. Just a teaspoon should do it.

7 Apply a **thin layer of Vaseline** around your hairline and your ears to keep from dying your skin along with your hair.

8 If you're doing your whole head, **divide your dry hair** into workable sections. Four will be good for short hair, but using six or more on longer hair will be helpful.

9   Use your tint brush to **work the Kool-Aid paste into your hair**, starting at the roots and going down the hair.

10 **Wrap the wet, Kool-Aided hair** (whether it's one piece or your whole head) in plastic wrap. Make sure to really wrap it up well because you're going to be sleeping on it! Alternatively, you could use a shower cap.

11 Use an old pillowcase or **wrap your pillow** in towels in case your plastic comes loose.

12 **Sleep on it!**

TIPS TO DYE FOR GOING STREAKING

If you're just doing a streak or one section, take the preferred piece of hair, paint your Kool-Aid paste onto the section and just be careful not to get it on the rest of your hair! If you hold some tinfoil under the part you're painting, that will really help. You can also pull all of your hair back in clips except for the part that you want dyed.

13 When you wake up, **wash out the dye with the coldest water** you can stand. It's okay if you can do no better than lukewarm, but don't use hot water! It opens the hair strands and all the color will drain right out. Don't use shampoo or conditioner for as long as possible, at least eight hours; the longer you go without them, the longer your color will hold!

14 Once you've rinsed the Kool-Aid out, **you're done!**

A VERY KOOL DIP DYE

Another option for making your hair super-Kool is to dip it in some steamy drink. Here's how:

MATERIALS FOR A DIP DYE

- Old T-shirt and towels
- Rubber gloves
- 2 packets of unsweetened Kool-Aid
- Small pot
- Water
- Heatproof bowl

INSTRUCTIONS THAT ARE SO KOOL, THEY'RE HOT

1 Put on an old T-shirt and put some old towels down to protect your work surface.

2 Empty 2 packets of Kool-Aid into a pot and fill the pot ½ way with water.

3 Bring the Kool-Aid water to a boil, stirring to dissolve the Kool-Aid powder.

4 Let the mixture cool until it is just barely steaming.

5 BE SO SUPER CAREFUL!! as you pour the mixture into a heatproof bowl.

6 Wrap an old towel around your shoulders. You can use a hair clip to hold it in place.

7 Dip your hair into the mixture for 5–10 minutes. You can just do the tips or dip as much as you want into the bowl. You'll never get to the roots, but you can get a really cool ombre this way.

8 Remove your hair from the mixture and let it air dry.

9 Rinse with cold water, dry again, and enjoy!

If your hair was dark originally, the Kool-Aid will likely just tint your hair. However, lighter base colors can be dramatically morphed! Like anything else having to do with hair, experimentation is your best friend.

COLORED-HAIRSPRAY TECHNIQUES

Even though making your own dye is really fun and personalized (and there's something to be said about avoiding the ingredients in any premade dye), you can get a lot of joy from using colored hairsprays and the endless techniques, colors, and blends to accentuate your base color.

While often used as a quickie Halloween alternative to scratchy wigs, colored hairspray isn't just for mimicking a witch. With the right brands and techniques, you can create a glam look that's perfect for a night on the town! Most hairsprays will wash out in one shampoo, but, as stated before, the more color-treated, porous, and damaged your hair is, the more likely the color will stick it out longer.

As with other bleach-free methods, applying spray in shades darker than your natural hair color will work much better than applying lighter shades on darker hair. A brunette trying to spray-paint her hair blond is going to have a hard time getting much of anything (that she likes, anyway) to show up. You can try spraying your hair white first and then adding color; just know that this isn't an exact science and that experimentation is your best friend when trying to find the best fit for you and your hair. Those with super-long or super-curly hair will also have a hard time, though nothing is impossible!

In my humble opinion, blondes look great with pink spray. Blue looks awesome on redheads (but may not do much for someone with dark hair). Purple works well on people with darker hair, since it gives an awesome two-tone look that makes people do a double take—especially in the light!

- Old T-shirt and towels
- Rubber gloves (optional}
- Colored hairspray
- Shampoo
- Several large hair clips
- Comb or brush

1. You'll have to **choose which kind** of colored hairspray to buy. Do your homework and purchase the best brand and colors for you and whatever effect you're looking to gain. Read all of the warnings and instructions before you buy so that you're familiar with the product you're using.

2. **Wash your hair with shampoo** and either let it air-dry or work it dry with a towel. While there has been debate about this depending upon the type of dye you're using, colored hairspray tends to work better on clean hair that is free of oils and dirt that could prevent the color from adhering to the surface of the hair strands.

TIPS TO DYE FOR
DIY SHOWER CAP HACK

You can employ a shower cap to protect the hair you're not dyeing, and this is especially easy to work with if you're just doing a front section or the back of your head. Looking for something really interesting to experiment with? Consider snipping holes into a shower cap and pull sections of hair through the holes (just like they used to do in salons before the days of foils to create highlights) to create asymmetrical stripes all over as you paint.

3 **Prep your space.** Lay down towels and wear an old T to prevent accidentally dyeing your countertop or favorite shirt. You can don some disposable gloves, but most sprays wash off the skin pretty easily. It's what they're designed to do!

4 **Make sure your hair is detangled and smooth.**

5 Decide what you want to spray and **divide your hair** based on your preference. Just doing one chunk near the front of your face? Tie and pin back the rest of your hair. Looking to do different colors in different sections? Separate everything with a comb and leave down only the first part that you'll be working with. It's best to work in small sections. It'll take longer, but you're less likely to mess up or suffer bleed-throughs on other parts of your scalp where you don't want that color.

6 Once you're all prepped and ready to go, shake your spray can and hold it about four to ten inches away from the section that you're spraying first. Covering your whole head in one shade? Hold it out a bit farther. **Color should be applied in quick bursts**, over and over, until you've fully saturated the area (not to the point of dripping wet, just until you're sure you've covered the section thoroughly).

7 Finish all of your sections, trying to keep each section separated as they dry—**bonus points if you waited for each section to dry** before moving on!—and then style to your liking. The color should be smooth and not sticky.

Voilà! You've got a short-term brand-new look.

GOT BANGS?

Getting the back of your head can be hard to do. If you're dyeing solo, you can easily add an awesome pop of color to just your bangs. Make sure they're combed out smoothly, and back your hair with some tinfoil so you don't spray yourself in the face (duh).

HOMEMADE HAIRSPRAY

Save money and ditch gross toxins by making your own hairspray. You won't believe how cheap and simple it is to make alcohol-free (alcohol dries out your hair!) spray. And it works—I swear!

MATERIALS

1 cup filtered water
Small saucepan
4 teaspoons sugar (less if you need less strength; more if you're looking for Superman-strength hold)
6 to 8 drops essential oil (optional, but suggested if you enjoy pleasant scents)
Funnel
Spray bottle
Makes 1 cup

MAKING THE SPRAY

1 Bring the water to a boil in a small saucepan.

2 Add sugar and stir to dissolve. Remove pan from the heat.

3 Cool completely and then add any essential oils.

4 Using a funnel, pour the mixture into the spray bottle.

5 Get rid of those flyaways!

HENNA RECIPES AND TECHNIQUES

Henna is one of the most popular natural ways to dye your hair. You can go the inexpensive and super-effective route of buying a block of henna dye from a place like LUSH Cosmetics and doing it that way, but I also want to show you a way to make your own henna dye and the best way to apply it.

Because of its natural properties, henna not only changes your hair color to gorgeous shades of red, it also conditions your hair really well and gives it a shiny and soft look—minus the chemicals found in salon dyes. It also helps protect against oily hair, helps remove dandruff, and helps prevent itchy scalp. It's an all-around winner! Henna is also available in brown, which is a great option if you want to enrich your already brown hair or cover up some grays.

However, henna dye is more permanent than the other dyes in this book. While anything and everything fades over time, you'll be stuck with the effects of red henna dye for a while longer. Of course, it's impossible to say how long, since it will depend on the current state of your hair when you dye, but just be aware that henna is a bit more, uh, sticky.

Also note that henna in its purest and truest form will turn your hair one color: red! Any other "henna" product that promises you another shade is mixed with something else. It's anyone's guess as to whether those added things are good or bad for your hair, so it's best to either stick with the original or be very careful about what you buy. To find true henna, scour Indian shops (the cheapest option) or all-natural beauty shops. The powder you're after should be a light algae green.

There are a number of different effects you can get from henna. Depending on how you use it, you can add a tinge of red that will shimmer in the sun, or you can go deep for the color of a dark red rose.

MATERIALS

- 8 tablespoons henna powder
- 2 cups boiling water
  (but you won't need it all)
- Disposable bowl

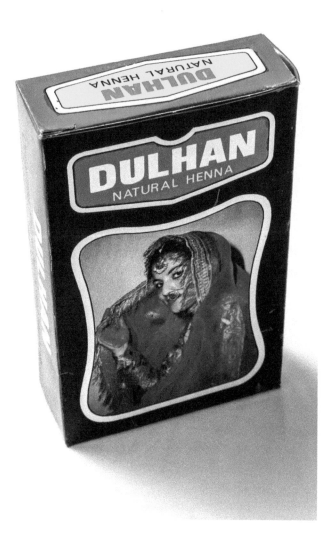

MAKING BASIC HENNA PASTE

1 **Boil water.**

2 **Put henna powder into a heatproof bowl.**

3 BE SO SUPER CAREFUL!! As you add the boiling water 1 tablespoon at a time to the henna powder, mixing as you go, until the consistency becomes a **thick paste, like a stiff cake batter.** (Don't let it get runny! But don't fret if it does. Just add more powder.)

4 **Let the mixture stand** for at least twelve hours.

If you're unsure whether or not you've prepared it correctly, you can do a test by putting a dollop of the mixture on your wrist. Rinse it off after about a minute. If the henna is in good shape, it'll stain your skin slightly yellow.

THE MANY SHADES OF HENNA

If red is what you're after but you're not into the typical henna red, there are tons of herbs and other natural ingredients that you can use to alter the standard red hue. Want to go as dark as possible? Indigo powder is great for that—about a tablespoon should do it.

Ingredients typically combined with henna to create great effects are:

- Intensified color: cloves, brandy
- Less intense color (more brown): coffee, black tea
- Darker color: nettles, walnut extract, indigo
- Lighter, more golden tones: anything acidic such as lemon juice, vinegar, red wine

The liquid ingredients can be swapped out for the water (entirely or just a little bit, depending on what you're after). With your base of dry ingredients, infuse and strain the added ingredients, then apply to hair. The color will fade after a couple of washes. To keep up with a favorite look, just keep repeating the same steps you took to get there every week or so.

Let's start dyeing!

MATERIALS

- Old towel or T-shirt
- Gloves
- Vaseline
- Henna paste
- Tint brush (optional)
- Plastic wrap, aluminum foil, or shower cap
- Conditioner

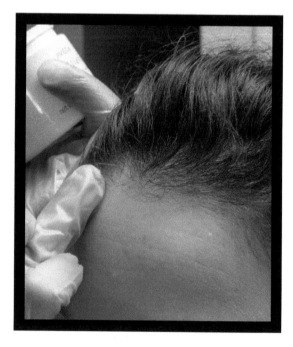

HAIR WE GO!

1. **Prep yourself and your work area** by donning an old T, putting on gloves, laying down an old towel so you don't stain any surfaces, and draping a final towel over your shoulders.

2. Apply **a thin layer of Vaseline** around your hairline and on your ears to keep from dyeing your skin along with your hair.

3. If you're doing your whole head, **divide your hair** into as many sections as you need to make it easy to work with. Four should be good for short hair, and six should work for long, thicker hair.

4. Apply henna paste to your hair generously using your hands, or a brush if you prefer. **Start at the roots** and work your way to the tips.

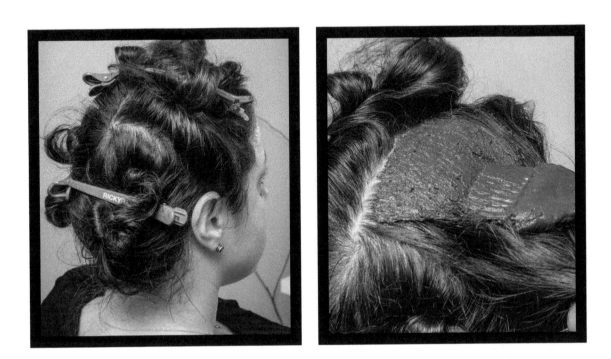

5 Wrap some plastic, aluminum foil, or a shower cap around your hair. **Let it stand** for at least an hour. The longer you have the mixture on, the more color you will get.

6 Once you've reached the hue you want, **apply conditioner** to your hair, massage, and rinse it all out with as cold of water as you can stand.

Don't freak out if the color is a bit orange-y at first. It may take a few days for the color to settle in. If you have any extra henna paste, freeze it and use for your next dye job!

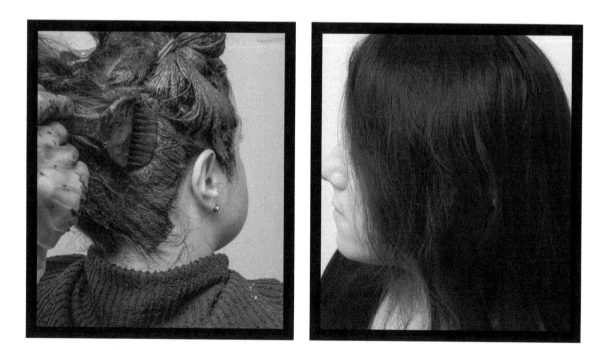

HENNA GLOSS

If you're looking for a subdued effect, gloss might work best for you. Gloss takes light hair to a red shimmer with the same added benefits of conditioning and strengthening the strands.

MATERIALS

- Old T-shirt and towels
- 2 tablespoons of henna paste (see above)
- Conditioner or yogurt
- Gloves
- Vaseline
- Plastic wrap, aluminum foil, or shower cap

DYEING HAIR WITH GLOSS

1 **Add henna** paste to your favorite conditioner or yogurt.

2 **Prep yourself and your work area** by donning an old T, putting on gloves, laying down an old towel so you don't stain any surfaces, and draping a final towel over your shoulders.

3 Apply **a thin layer of Vaseline** around your hairline and on your ears to keep from dyeing your skin along with your hair.

4 **Apply the henna paste to towel-dried hair** and cover.

5 **Leave on** for at least thirty minutes.

6 Rinse and let hair **air-dry.**

TEA BAGS AND OTHER HIPPIE METHODS

It doesn't get anymore hippie DIY than using tea to color your hair! Though the concept is super fun, I should caution you that these methods are the most shaky to use. While they definitely have the ability to work well to a certain extent, they're a less tried-and-true method for dyeing hair. But, if you can get it to work on your base color, it's just about the most green and eco-friendly way to change up your hair color. Below, I will outline the different methods and teas to try based on your base color. These should only last until you shampoo your hair. For the best results, rinse your hair with cold water to seal the color and let your hair air dry once you're done applying.

For all of these methods, your basic workspace prep should include putting on an old T-shirt, laying old towels around where you will be doing the dyeing, and draping another towel over your shoulders.

FOR BLONDIES

All-Over Color
This is a great recipe for all-over color enhancement.

    6 chamomile tea bags
    ½ cup plain yogurt
    Lavender oil
    Tint brush
    Shower cap or plastic wrap

1 Bring water to a boil and steep the tea for 15 minutes in a large pot.

2 Once the tea has cooled down (but is not cold), mix it with the yogurt and lavender oil and let it rest until it reaches a temperature you're comfortable putting on your head.

3 Use a tint brush to apply the mixture to dry hair, starting at the top and working your way to the ends.

4 Once your hair is fully saturated, cover your head in a shower cap or some plastic wrap and sit for 30 minutes.

5 Rinse your hair when the time is up, but don't shampoo and avoid using a hairdryer if you can.

Highlights
If you're looking for natural highlights, you can use this method to give your whole head a fun tint or section off a few pieces (though that is harder for this type of recipe).

    1 cup lemon juice
    3 cups chamomile tea

1 Bring water to a boil and steep the tea for 15 minutes in a large pot.

2 Once the tea has cooled down (but is not cold) add the lemon juice and tea and let it rest until it reaches a temperature you're comfortable putting on your head.

3 Pour it all over your hair.

4 Go outside and sit in the sun for an hour, getting as much direct sunlight on your hair as possible.

5 Head back inside to rinse and condition your hair, but don't shampoo it.

BRUNETTE

All-Over Color

This is an awesome way to make your hair color richer.

  1 large pot of brewed black tea or coffee

1 Brew a large pot of coffee or black tea.

2 Let the liquid cool down to lukewarm, so it's easy to handle.

3 Saturate your dry hair thoroughly with the liquid by pouring it all over your hair and catching it in a large bowl or pot for later use.

4 Right after, rinse it out and shampoo your hair.

5 Now rinse with your drink again.

6 Keep rinsing several more times—each time will make your hair darker—but skip the shampoo all but the first time.

7 Leave the final rinse in your hair for at least 15 minutes.

8 Rinse with cold water.

RED

All-Over Color

  Rosehips
  Cloves
  5 cups water

1 Brew rose hips and cloves in the water, as you would a tea.

2 Let the liquid cool down to lukewarm, so it's easy to handle.

3 Saturate your dry hair thoroughly with the liquid by pouring it all over your hair and catching it in a large bowl or pot for later use.

4 Right after, rinse it out and shampoo your hair.

5 Now rinse with your drink again.

6 Keep rinsing several more times—each time will make your hair darker—but skip the shampoo all but the first time.

7 Leave the final rinse in your hair for at least 15 minutes.

8 Rinse with cold water.

FOOD-COLORING RECIPES AND TECHNIQUES

Like colored hairspray, food coloring will most likely wash out the first time you take a shower. But if you love the results, you can lengthen your next dye job by using developer from a beauty supply store such as Sally Beauty Supply.

While Kool-Aid is known for creating awesome red hair on many a crafty girl, food-coloring dyes open the door to just about any color you'd like to experiment with. It bears repeating that the shade of your dye job and how long it sticks will totally depend on the current color and state of your hair. For instance, a brunette or dirty blonde using blue dye will likely receive a more navy effect. Got blond hair? Lucky you, that hair is gonna be BLUE. Like, Smurf blue. But if you can dig it, so can I!

MATERIALS

- Old T-shirt and towels
- Rubber gloves
- Liquid food coloring
- Small bowl
- Tint brush
- Vaseline
- Conditioner (optional)
- Tin foil (optional)
- Comb
- Blow dryer
- Hairspray or gel

TIPS TO DYE FOR ALL THE COLORS OF THE RAINBOW

Most of the time you can only find food coloring in the primary colors with maybe a green thrown in there. If you're looking for something like purple, just pull out that kindergarten color wheel—you'll need to mix blue and red.

INSTRUCTIONS FOR FOOD DYE HAIR DYE

1 Put on an **old T-shirt and gloves**. Lay old towels down around where you'll be dyeing, and drape one over your shoulders.

2 Pour your food coloring **into a small bowl** so it's easy to get at with a tint brush. You can mix it with a bit of conditioner—about a teaspoon—if you want to soften the color. This will also make the mixture pasty and easier to work with.

3 Apply **a thin layer of Vaseline** around your hairline and on your ears to keep from dyeing your skin along with your hair.

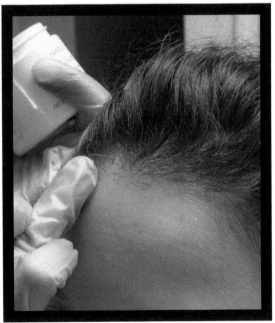

4 If you're doing your whole head, **divide your hair** into workable sections. Four will be good for short hair, but using six or more on longer hair will be helpful.

5 **Apply the food coloring** to the hair using a tint brush starting near the roots and working your way to the tips.

6 If you're doing only one or just a few parts, remember to pull the other sections back with clips! You may want to **paint the sections you're dyeing against some tinfoil** to keep the dye from getting on other parts of your hair.

7 **Air-dry** your hair, or blow-dry on a low setting.

8 **Spray on some hairspray or put some gel on** to style your hair and lock the dye in a bit.

This dye is one that WILL get on everything. So take extra caution while you're putting it into your hair. And if you run your hand through your hair or sleep on it, be prepared for your hand and your pillowcase to match your hair.

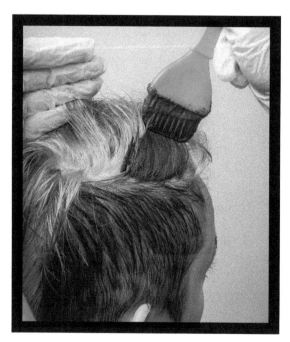

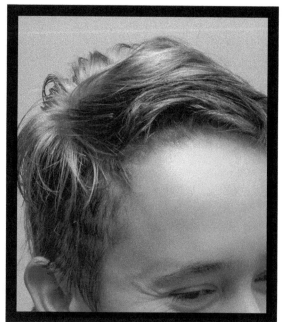

If you're nervous, consider doing the whole process on just one strand to see how you like the shade. Once you've got it down, brush and section your hair. If you're doing a partial job, you'll want to tie up any sections you aren't dyeing. Even if you're doing your whole head, it'll be easier to break it down by section and work around your head one section at a time.

GLITTER HAIR GEL

Looking for a nontoxic way to hold your new colored 'do in place? Save money and get crafty with a homemade glitter hair gel that will have your strands looking smooth with just a touch of sparkle! This solution dries to a hard hold but can easily wash out if you make a mistake or want the look temporarily. The gel is inexpensive and so simple to make that you'll wonder why you haven't been doing it for years.

Psst: Want the hair gel but not the glitter? Just skip that ingredient.

MATERIALS:

- 2½ cups water
- 1 tablespoon unflavored gelatin
- 4 tablespoon glitter, nontoxic, any color

MAKING THE GEL

1. In a small saucepan, boil the water.

2. Add the gelatin and stir until dissolved.

3. Let mixture cool to room temperature.

4. If you want to use glitter, add it now.

5. Refrigerate for at least two hours. The mixture will gel while in the fridge, so be sure to stir it before using it on your hair.

When it's ready to use, simply apply it to your hair however you like! You can make beach waves, finger curls, Mohawks, or sleek styles with the gel, and you'll only need to use a little to get what you're going for. Remember that it holds strong, so too much gel is going to A) create a glitter mess and B) make your hair so dry it's stabby.

STORE-BOUGHT COLORING TECHNIQUES

When all is said and done, even with all of the funky, natural DIY options available, there are going to be times when you just require a tub or box of store-bought color. These include times where you're in rush, in a pinch, or want a color that's going to last. You can pick up a tub of semi-permanent cream dye such as Manic Panic, which has been fashioning zingy colors for decades. Or you can get some really awesome eggplants and burgundies from traditional brands like L'Oreal.

No matter what your reasons are, there is no sin in buying prepackaged color. The package instructions shouldn't lead you astray (it's definitely one of the easier forms of color transformation), but I still have some tips for my favorite dye-job-at-home process.

- Old T-shirt and towels
- Rubber gloves
- Store-bought dye
- Vaseline
- Small disposable bowl
- Tint brush
- Aluminum foil (optional)
- Comb

LET'S GET CRAZY

1. Wash and dry your hair but **DO NOT condition it**.

2. Put on an **old T-shirt and gloves**. Lay old towels down around where you'll be dyeing, and drape one over your shoulders.

3. Apply **a thin layer of Vaseline** around your hairline and on your ears to keep from dyeing your skin along with your hair.

4 **Pour the dye into the bowl**—it'll be easier to scoop the dye out than from the original container.

5 If you're doing your whole head, **divide your hair** into workable sections. Four will be good for short hair, but using six or more on longer hair will be helpful.

6 Using the tint brush, paint the dye onto your hair **starting about half an inch from your scalp,** or wherever you would like the dye to start, and begin working your way down.

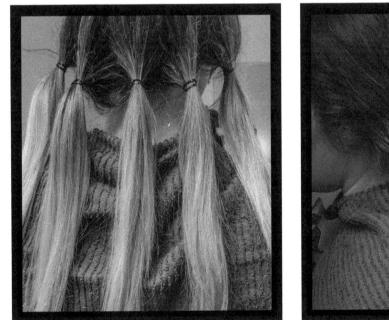

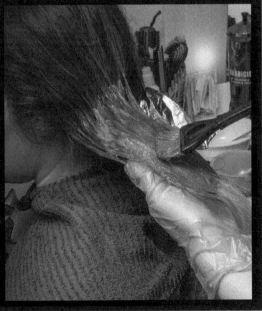

7 If you're not doing your whole head or you're using multiple colors, you may want to **paint the dye on using some aluminum foil as backing** to paint on and wrap your hair in so you don't rope in unsuspecting hairs. If you are dyeing your whole head, you can use your hands to scoop the dye onto your hair and really get it on every strand.

8 Comb the color through your hair and **get a good froth going**.

✄ TIPS TO DYE FOR ✄
HEAT BLAST

Some say using a little heat from a blow dryer will help the color set faster and become more intense. Give it a shot if you want, but it's not essential.

9 Now just **sit back and relax** for thirty to sixty minutes.

10 Rinse your hair with cold water and **do your thing! Air-dry or blow-dry** to see the final result, which might look different than it does wet.

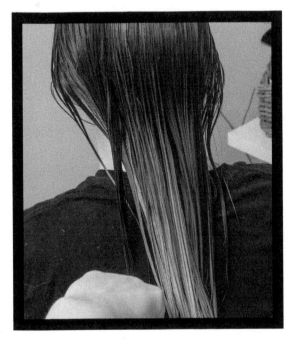

KNOW YOUR BOX DYE

There are two types of box colors. A semi-permanent color (which is applied to damp hair) is best for slight changes. Permanent color is the right choice for a full-on change. Of course, permanent color is a longer commitment, too, as it will often take up to six weeks (or about twenty washes) to wash out.

You can find box colors at your local grocery store, but I suggest hitting up an actual beauty supply shop for more options.

You can choose to go lighter or darker than wherever you're at, though I wouldn't suggest going too crazy different at once. A few shades darker or lighter usually yields the best results at home.

It's easy to get distracted by the little locks of fake hair below each box, showing you the finished hair color, but remember that the color sample was likely based on a start color of blond. You'll need to check out the side of the box to see the effects of the color on your base color. Don't see your current color? Try to find a color that includes your base color on the side, as you'll likely be most happy with those results. Once you've got your box at home, deep-condition your hair a couple of days before you plan to dye. You'll want to wash your hair the day or night before you dye, but I wouldn't suggest doing it the same day.

READY TO DYE?

1 Be sure to thoroughly read the instructions on your box before starting.

2 Put on an old T-shirt and gloves and lay down old towels.

3 Take the first section and squeeze the dye out of the bottle at your roots (about a quarter inch from your scalp), fully saturating the whole section. You can simply run your fingers through the strands to get both sides. If you're not doing your whole head you may want to paint the dye on using some aluminum foil as backing to paint on and wrap your hair in so you don't rope in unsuspecting hairs.

4 Repeat this for each section you're coloring.

5 Set a timer or alarm for the amount of time suggested on your box. You'll want to allow the specified time for your color to develop, and I don't suggest going under or over, even if it looks like the color isn't quite right. (You can always redye or touch up later, but you don't want to damage your hair or risk thinking it looks one way only to find out after you wash and blow dry it that you left it on too long.)

6 Shampoo your hair. Often, your box will come with a special shampoo. Use this, and continue to use it for your next few shampoos if you have extra after your initial wash.

OMBRE AND THEN SOME

If you want to add color after you bleach into an ombre, you can get some really vivid tones.

Don't feel like you have to stick to just a two-tone. You *can* begin the color right at the blond, but you can also go up into the color above the bleach line or start lower and leave a strip of blond peeking through for a pronounced 3-color effect.

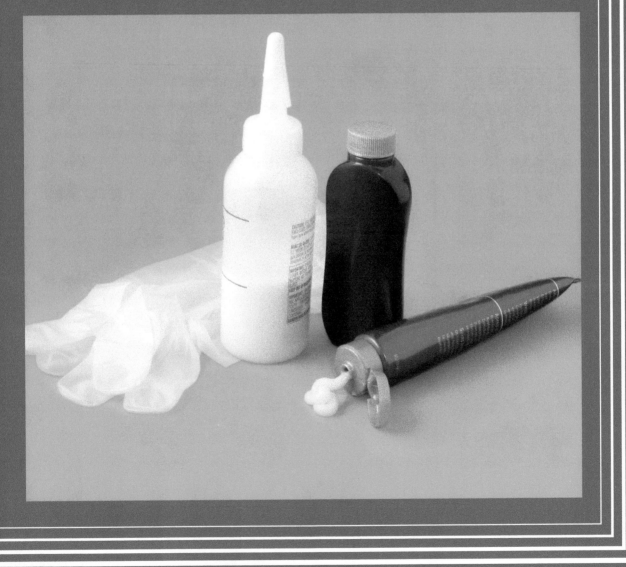

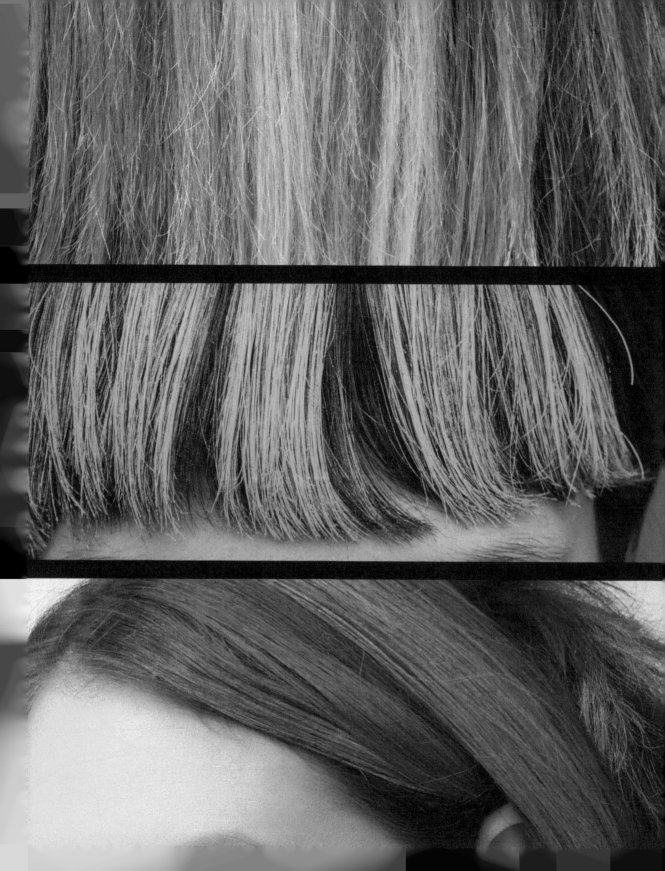

DIY STYLE

JUST AS THERE ARE TONS OF OPTIONS FOR DYES
AND COLORS, THERE ARE ALSO SO MANY STYLES
YOU CAN USE TO TRICK OUT YOUR TRESSES.

FULL HEAD

Doing your whole head one color may seem like a lot of work, but it's actually one of the easiest things to do! Because you won't have to section your hair extensively to keep the color from getting on the wrong parts, it's a lot faster and less harried to apply the dye. While the exact method might vary a little with each way of coloring (see the separate chapters on specific types of dye), below is a general outline for coloring your whole head.

First, you'll need to choose a method and a color. Once you've decided, you can move forward with the appropriate steps based on your choice. If you're doing a more permanent coloring (like store-bought boxed dye), you'll want to deep-condition your hair a couple of days before you plan to dye. You'll also want to wash your hair the day or night *before* you dye, but I wouldn't suggest doing it the same day.

Before you dye, be sure to read the instructions carefully for your chosen method. If you're going with box dye— even if you've done it before—be sure to read everything before starting. If you're nervous, consider doing the whole process on just one strand to see how you like the shade.

1 **Brush and section your hair** into four to six parts. Even when you're doing your whole head, it's be easier to break it down by section and work around your head one section at a time.

2 Take the first section (I often find that it's best to start at the back and work my way around to the front, but if a friend is doing the dyeing, the opposite is true) and **apply the dye** at your roots, fully saturating the whole section.

3 **Repeat this for each section** you're coloring.

4 **Set a timer** or alarm for the amount of time you'll need to sit with your color on. You'll want to allow the specified time for your color to develop. I don't suggest going under or over, even if it looks like the color isn't quite right. (You can always re-dye or touch up later, but you don't want to damage your hair or risk thinking it looks one way only to find out after you wash and blow-dry it that you left it on too long.)

5 Once your time is up, **wash out the dye** using the prescribed method for the dye you chose.

6 **Air-dry or blow-dry** your hair to see the final result, which might look different than it does wet.

If you love it, you can use the same dye method to touch up your roots in a few weeks' time. Remember to use a shampoo for color-treated hair specific to the color you're trying to keep in your hair! If you don't love it, you can experiment with a different hue or toners in about a week. Try not to wash it during that time.

Each type of hair color will last a different amount of time—from just a day up until twenty washes or more! With all the colors and methods out there, you shouldn't have any trouble finding the perfect way to color your whole head!

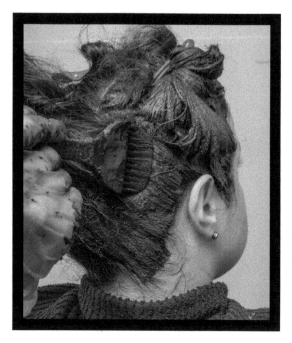

STREAKS, HIGHLIGHTS, AND LOWLIGHTS

Streaks, highlights, and lowlights are a super-popular way to add dimension to your at-home hair color. No matter the method you use—store-bought dye, Kool-Aid, hair chalk, etc.—it gives your hair a lift. You can accent your current color with a lighter, brighter hue in the same color family (highlights), add depth with a darker hue (lowlights), or branch entirely with a funky pop of pink, green, or whatever (streaks). No matter which way you go, putting some strips of color into your hair is a sure way to add some fun to your 'do.

HIGHLIGHT HELPER

If you're looking for highlights that will complement your natural hair and thinking of doing highlights with boxed color, you'll want to pick up a box specifically for root coverage. You can buy a highlighting kit, but I've often found that "root coverage" kits work better. For the "standard" highlight look, you'll want a color that is two to three shades lighter than the color your current hair is. So, if your hair is light to dark blond, you'll be looking for a kit that can add pale, beige-blonde highlights. If your hair is currently light brown, you might consider going for dark blond or caramel streaks. Medium brown hair looks great with golden-brown highlights. But these are just ideas! You should experiment with shades that get you excited and that you think will mesh well with your base color. If you have black or red hair, be extra careful when selecting highlight colors, as they won't really be "highlights" as much as just adding a new color to certain areas of your mane, which are more like streaks.

LOWLIGHT LOWDOWN

For the "standard" lowlight look, you'll want a color that is two to three shades darker than your current color. Blondes can try a deeper shade of blond or a light brown. "Honey" or "caramel" is what you're looking for here. Brunettes can opt to choose rich brown and red shades. Or "cinnamon" or auburn. If you've got pale skin, you're better off going with copper and auburn tones, as these will compliment your face. Redheads can go super-simple and just choose other shades of red. If you want to stand out a bit more, you could also try golden brown or brunette tones, just know that these are going to be a bit "louder." Again, these are just ideas. Pick what gets you jazzed!

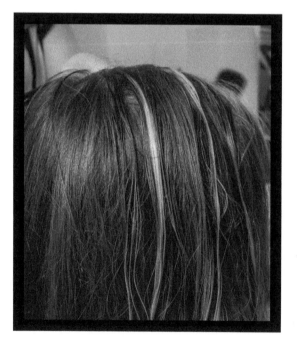

Prep by getting all of your essentials in order, including your chosen dye, an old T-shirt, hair ties and clips, and a towel to keep your work area clean. Read through the instructions for the kind of dye you're using, so you know what you're doing.

If you're at all worried about your color pick, consider doing a test strand to make sure you like what you see. If your color turns out too light, you can try again with a slightly darker dye. If the color isn't light enough, you can try applying more dye to the section, waiting another five minutes, and checking to see what you think. Once you've got something you love, you know exactly what you'll need to do in order to execute it for your whole head.

1 Thoroughly **brush your hair**.

2 Pull half your hair up and **clip it**.

3 Pull about **eight random pieces** of hair that are about two inches away from each other out of the clip. You can choose your targeted strands as you pull them off your head. Be sure to choose a few pieces close to your face and don't forget the back of your head. If you need help reaching all the way around, consider asking a friend or family member to help you before you start dyeing.

4 Once you know which pieces you want to dye, you can let your hair down (which will let you get to the roots of the pieces you're dyeing) and start to **apply the dye**.

5 Work slowly from the back to the front of your head, **coloring all sides of the strands**.

6 You can simply take the section and clip it back up when you're done applying the dye, or **if you're worried about making a mess, use foils**! Hold a piece of aluminum foil under each section and paint the dye onto it, on top of the foil. Then, fold the foil up as you may have seen done in salons. This way, you've got no worries that the color is touching the rest of your head!

7 Once you're done, sit (with a shower cap over your head if you like) for the suggested time for your method. **The longer you sit,** the more intense the color will be. If you're using bleach or a box highlight or lowlight, I wouldn't suggest going over the allotted time. You can always redo it if you aren't happy with the results.

8 When the time is up, **wash your work out and blow-dry** your hair to see the results!

If you like what you see, you know that you can use the same method and color again and again in the future.

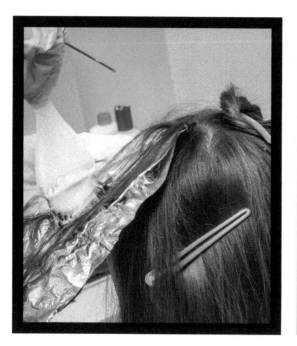

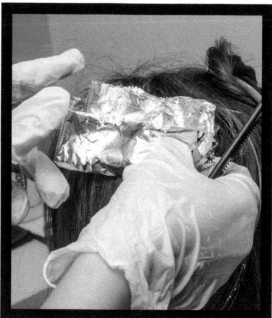

If you'd like to try a more natural touch-up method, consider one of these:

Lemon juice: Are you a blondie? Keep your shade popping by simply mixing equal parts lemon juice and water in a spray bottle and spraying it onto your roots. It tends to work best if you follow up by hanging out in the sun for about forty-five minutes before washing it out.

Chamomile: If you've got blond highlights and want a lightening effect, you can make some chamomile tea and use an applicator brush to apply it to your roots. Leave it on for around thirty minutes before washing it out.

Cinnamon: If you've got red or auburn highlights, you can use cinnamon to keep your color in line. Make a paste with ground cinnamon and water (add the water slowly until you get a pasty consistency) and apply it to your roots. Leave it in for thirty minutes and then rinse it out.

OMBRE

Ombre—it's the fad that won't go away. Not that I mind, since I've been sporting some version of it for more than two years now. At the time, I was looking to finally mature my hairstyle and coloring a bit. For me, ombre is the perfect way to maintain a little bit of fun in my more "grown-up" hairstyling. Even if you're just doing the most conventional version—brown on top, blond on bottom—you can play with the shading and get a really fun look. Or you can fade from brown to purple, black to blue, purple to pink—any combo you like! Just be sure to think about how the colors will run into each other before you start putting dye to hair.

And while it may seem like a tough style to nab at home, it's really not! In fact, if you're super-nervous for whatever reason, L'Oreal recently came out with an ombre kit called Féria Wild Ombre, with a "brush-on ombre effect." It'd be hard to mess that one up. If you want to go that route, I won't hold it against you.

Below are my instructions for fading from darker on top to lighter at the bottom. If you want the opposite look, you'll need to use these instructions for your roots and either leave your already-dark hair untreated at the bottom or dye it dark.

You may just want to go from your natural color to blond, in which case you'll just want to do a bleach job with the instructions on the next page. If you want to go for some fun colors, you can do the dye after you bleach into an ombre but let your hair rest for a week after you bleach it before you dye it. Or you can dye on top of whatever base color you already have, but as I talked about before, the results will vary based on the color you start with and the dye you use.

OMBRE WE GO!

As usual, you'll first want to prep your hair and your space. Make sure your hair is dry and brushed, and that your space is covered with old towels in case of spillage. Sport an old T-shirt and use gloves. If you've got windows in your bathroom, open them to help with ventilation.

1. Thoroughly **brush out** your hair, and then tease the part you want to ombre. This will give a nice color transition and prevent you from having a hard line of color change.

TIPS TO DYE FOR
20/20 BLEACHING INTO AN OMBRE

If you are bleaching out your bottom to get an ombre, you will want to use a 20 volume peroxide and leave the bleach on for twenty minutes—no more!—depending on how light you want to go. If you're looking for a barely there change, you can wash out after ten minutes. You'll be able to see your hair changing right before your eyes, but just remember that wet hair looks different than dry hair, so don't freak out if it isn't processing the way you'd expected.

TIPS TO DYE FOR
DEFEAT THE BLEACH

Whenever bleach is involved in getting your favorite color, consider coating your hair in organic coconut oil and sleeping on it at least once a month. The coconut oil returns some of the nutrients that the bleach stripped away. Remember: As awesome as bleach is for attaining your dream color, it's still really hard on your hair.

2. **Section off your hair** into manageable chunks (I'd go with four). Don't worry about making them especially even; ombre isn't an exact science!

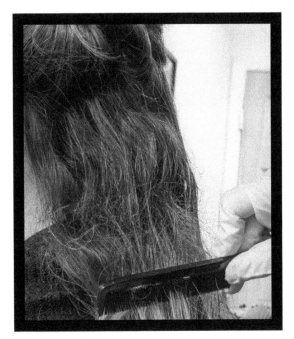

3 Use a tint brush to apply the dye or bleach to the ends of your hair **in a downward motion**. You can do this against foils or an old towel—either way, it'll help to have something to hold your hair against as you paint on the mixture.

4 Do this for each section, starting **as high up on your strands as you like**. Some prefer very little ombre at the top (basically a "just the tips" look) and others go to the halfway point. There is no right or wrong answer. If you're unsure, I'd suggest going from the height of your mouth down. Once you know how far up you want to go, the most important thing is to repeat that same cutoff on each section.

5 When you've completed each section, **consider redoing the tips** if you'd like an obvious boldness there at the bottom.

6 **Leave the dye on** for as long as the method specifies. If you're bleaching, don't go longer than twenty minutes.

7 Once your time is up, **wash the mixture out of your hair** and air-dry or blow-dry and style. If you're happy, you've found your go-to method for ombre.

If you wish the ombre was lighter/darker/ went up higher on your strands, etc., you've now learned a valuable lesson for next time! Give your hair a break for a week and then get back to experimenting. You can also tone your hair if it's at all yellow-y or orange-y. If you have all blond hair and need to take your top half darker, you can simply buy an appropriate box color shade and just do your roots down to your ombre.

OMBRE AND THEN SOME

If you want to add color after you bleach into an ombre, you can get some really vivid tones.

Don't feel like you have to stick to just a two-tone. Experiment by dyeing above the bleach line, or start lower and leave a strip of blond peeking through for a pronounced 3-color effect.

JUST THE TIPS

Looking to do red, purple, or a light shade? If you're blond, you can go ahead and just dye right on top of your base. If you've got darker hair and want lighter tips (but not blond), you'll need to bleach first and then add the color that you want to attain. You can use the method on the following pages for bleaching, dyeing, or bleaching and then dyeing. Remember, it's good to let your hair rest at least a week between bleaching it out and dyeing.

If you're bleaching, use "Tips to Dye For: 20/20 Bleaching into an Ombre," on page 79.

Prep yourself and your space. You should wear an old T-shirt and prep your workspace by laying down some old towels. Oh, and open a window so the fumes don't go to your head.

GETTING A NICE TIP

1 Thoroughly **brush your hair.**

2 You may want to **divide and clip your hair** into sections to make it easier to work with. Four sections should do the trick.

3 Take the first section of hair and (hold it against a piece of foil if you like) and **apply the color.**

4 Fold up your foil(s) and move onto the next section, **moving all the way around your head.**

5 **Once you're done,** sit with it on however long the method states. You can check the processing in the mirror, though the final result will look different once your hair is washed and dried.

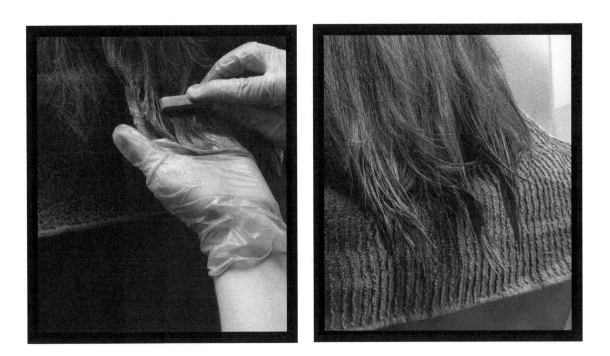

6 When the time's up, **wash out the dye** with the prescribed method for what you're doing.

7 **Blow-dry** and style your hair and you're golden! (Or pink, or whatever other funky color you chose.)

TIPS TO DYE FOR
YOU DON'T HAVE TO BE MONOCHROMATIC

If you'd like to do a rainbow effect on your tips, choose three colors, divide the sections of hair to be dyed into thirds, and apply three inches of color onto each third!

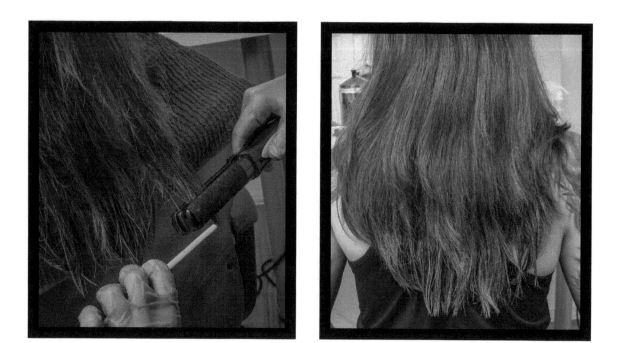

TWO-TONE

As ombre and "just the tips" styles have become as popular as highlights and lowlights, the definition of two-tone hair has become more muddled. Ask five different people for their opinions, and you may get a variety of answers. For me, two-tone is one color underneath and one color on top, and that's what I want to show you how to do now. This could be done by just dyeing one section if you already love your current color, but I'm going to go ahead and explain doing both colors. If you just want to do either your top or bottom, just follow that part of the instructions.

The first thing you have to do is decide on your shades. Are you doing two colors or just one? Can you dye directly onto your current shade or will you have to bleach first? For a simple and subtle change, you can pick dyes that are either close to what you already have or just a few shades apart, such as a dark blond on top and a light brown on the bottom. If you'd rather do something loud and proud, I've always loved platinum blond on top and purple underneath or black on top and bright red underneath. You do you!

If you're bleaching, do that first (see pages 19–23).

Prep your hair and your space. Make sure your space is covered with old towels. Wear an old T-shirt and use gloves. If you've got windows in your bathroom, open them to help with ventilation.

This example is a two-tone mohawk, with the mohawk one color and the sides their original color. The process is still pretty much the same though, and the text describes the more "traditional" style of doing two-tone on long hair.

ONE, TWO, GO!

1 **Brush your hair** thoroughly.

2 From the back of your head, **divide your hair** from the top and the bottom. Pull up the top portion and clip it. It's up to you how evenly you want to divide the hair. Just don't do so little on the bottom that it won't stand out at all!

3 You'll want to work on the bottom half first. **Apply the dye** starting at the roots and going down toward the tips. It may be easier to use your fingers, but you can also use a tint brush if you like.

4 Work this way around your entire head until the **bottom half is all coated.** Let it process however long it is recommended for your color.

5 **Rinse** but don't shampoo yet, even if the dye method calls for it.

6 **Clip the dyed portion of your hair** at the nape of your neck. Basically, keep it out of the way as cleanly as possible. You may want to wrap it in plastic wrap to keep the dye from touching other portions of your hair.

7 Now, **mix the dye** for your top half.

8 **Apply the dye,** starting from the part in your hair at the back of your head and working forward. Work slowly and meticulously—you do not want to get any dye from the top half on your bottom half! Leaning over the sink to work may help.

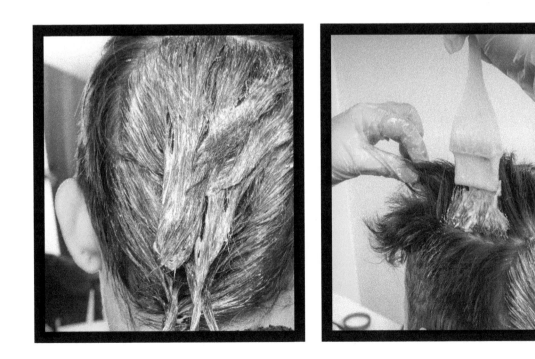

9 Once you're all covered, it's time for **the waiting game,** the rules of which are determined by the type of coloring you're using.

10 Once you've won the waiting game, **rinse the dye** from the top of your head without messing with the bottom portion. Then rinse the bottom portion.

11 Now, shampoo all of your hair to set the dyes if that's what the type of dye you're using calls for. Apply any special conditioners that may be part of your process. If you went blond in one section and need to tone, now's the time to go for it!

12 Otherwise, **blow-dry and style.** If you want to adjust the color, you can always go darker by redyeing with a darker hue in a week.

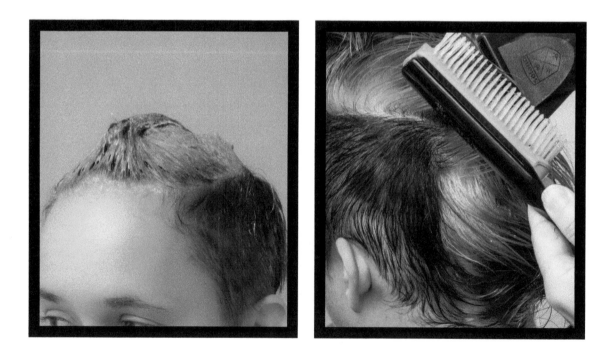

RAINBOW

Clearly, this is not for the faint of heart. Rainbow hair makes a statement. If you're looking to do rainbow tips, check out the Just the Tips section on pages 82–84. That's a great way to do something really loud and proud without going whole hog. But, if you're in it for the whole shebang, you'll want to bleach your whole head—unless you have white or platinum-blond hair (if so, lucky you!). See pages 19–23 for this step, and then return here once you're done.

You'll want to go ahead and choose which sections will get which colors before you do anything. It's totally up to you if you want four colors or six or eight (or anything in between). Arrange your bottles in front of you, so you can see the colors next to each other. Put them in an order that seems harmonious to you—think about how the colors blend together, as they will over time—and that's how you'll end up working around your head. In other words, I wouldn't suggest putting orange next to purple. Not a pretty combo, baby.

LET'S GO OVER THE RAINBOW!

1 Okay! You're bleached and ready to go. **Make sure your hair is dry,** brushed, and parted down the middle.

2 **Divide your hair into sections** around your head, separating based on when you'll want to change colors. Tie each section into its own elastic band or clip.

3 Using a tint brush, start at the front of your hairline and work your way back, **covering each section with dye** from roots (or wherever you want the dye to start) to ends.

4. Each time you finish a section, **wrap it in plastic wrap or foil** so that none of the colors bleed together in the dyeing process.

5. **Once you've applied the dye** to each section, you'll wrap all of your separate plastic bundles under a plastic shower cap, or you could just wrap more plastic wrap on top of everything.

6. Now you wait! Your colors and method will dictate your timing, but you'll probably want to give it **at least forty minutes.**

7. Once things are looking good, **rinse everything out** and condition, working out tangles with your fingers.

8 Next, you'll want to **put on a leave-in conditioner.** Let it air-dry and do not wash your hair for at least twenty-four hours. The longer you can go without an initial shampoo, the longer your colors will last.

TIPS TO DYE FOR
FOR THE LOVE OF PILLOWS

I'd suggest wrapping your pillow with a towel the first couple of nights so that you don't stain your pillowcase!

INDEX

B

Bangs, coloring, 42
Bleach, 17–23
    double processing hair before, 18
    guidelines for using, 12, 17
    high lift tint vs., 12
    at home vs. salon, 17
    lot of hair and, 20
    materials needed, 17, 19
    ombre and. *See* Ombre
    prepping hair, 19
    step-by-step instructions, 20–23
    tricky hair and, 18
Blond(es)
    changing hair to, before coloring, 17.
        See also Bleach
    coloring options, 10–11
    highlighting. *See* Highlights
    tea bags for, 52–53
Blue / purple hair, 11, 13, 55, 78
Brunettes
    coloring options, 11
    highlighting. *See* Highlights
    tea bags for, 53

C

Cautions, 13
Chalking, 25–29
    guidelines for using, 25
    materials needed, 25, 26
    recipe, 29
    step-by-step instructions, 26–28
Chamomile, 52, 77
Cinnamon, 77
Color
    amount/styles of. *See* Styles
    base, dyeing options, 10–11
    blond- or light-hair base options, 10–11
    brunette base options, 11
    dye expectations by, 13
    high lift, 12

Colored-hairspray techniques, 39–42
    base colors and, 39
    guidelines for using, 39
    materials needed, 40
    recipe for making, 43
    step-by-step instructions, 40–42
Cutting hair, stencils/designs and, 23

D

Developer, about, 18
Double process, 18
Duration, of colors, 13
Dye
    cautions, 13
    commercial. *See* Store-bought
        coloring techniques
    duration by color, 13
    testing effects, 59

F

Food coloring, 57–59
    coloring options, 57
    extending effects of, 57
    materials needed, 56
    step-by-step instructions, 57–59

G

Glitter hair gel, 59
Green hair, 13

H

Hair chalk. *See* Chalking
Hairspray. *See* Colored-hairspray techniques
Heat, to set color faster, 64
Henna, 45–51
    characteristics of, 45
    gloss, dyeing hair with, 51
    guidelines for using, 45
    making basic paste, 46–47
    materials needed, 46, 48

shades of, 45, 48
step-by-step techniques, 46, 49–50, 51
High lift color, 12
Highlights, 73–74, 75, 77

K

Kool-Aid, 31–37
   dipping hair in steamy drink, 37
   guidelines for using, 31
   materials needed, 32
   recipe, 37
   step-by-step instructions, 33–36
   streaking hair with, 35

L

Lemon juice, 52, 77
Lowlights, 73, 74–75

M

Materials needed, 10.
   See also specific techniques

N

Nourishing hair, toner for, 11

O

Ombre, 67, 78–81
Orange / yellow hair, 13

P

Pillows, protecting from color, 92
Pink / red hair, 13
Prepping hair, 19
Purple hair. *See* Blue / purple hair

R

Rainbow hair, 89–93
Redheads, tea bags for, 53
Red / pink hair, 13. *See also* Kool-Aid

S

Shower cap, for coloring sections, 40
Stenciling hair, 23
Store-bought coloring techniques
   about: overview of, 61
   box dyes, 66–67
   checking out color effects for
    base color, 66
   guidelines for using, 66
   materials for semi-permanent
    creams, 62
   setting color faster, 64
   step-by-step instructions,
    62–65, 66–67
   types of colors, 66
Streaks, 73, 75–76
Styles
   full head, 70–73
   ombre, 67, 78–81
   rainbow, 89–93
   streaks, highlights, lowlights, 73–77
   tips only, 82–83
   two-tone, 85–88

T

Tea bags, coloring with, 52–53
Testing dye, 59
Tips only, 82–83
Toner, characteristics/benefits, 11
Two-tone color, 85–88

Y

Yellow / orange hair, 13

ABOUT THE AUTHOR

Loren Lankford is a Georgia native, NYU film grad and current L.A. dweller. When she isn't rescuing dogs from high-kill shelters; thrifting items for her online shop, Southern Dropout; or editing her crafting website, CraftFoxes, she's doing actual freelance work! She has worked on the magazines *CosmoGIRL!*, *Cosmopolitan*, *Entertainment Weekly*, and *Jane*, and she has written, produced, and edited for AOL's Lemondrop.com, NBC's iVillage, *Paste Magazine*, MTV, and several others. She also helped launch Fab and Bookish. "Time off" means traveling all over the world for sporting events and film festivals—her most favorite things.

ABOUT THE HAIR STYLIST

Michelle Mumoli is an Aveda trained and licensed hair stylist as well as assistant director of Not Yo Mama's Craft Fair. She is based in downtown Jersey City, New Jersey.

ABOUT THE PHOTOGRAPHER

Jason Hofmann is a professional photographer in the New York City area. He has a wide range of freelance work experience that includes portraiture, panoramic landscapes, sporting events, and everything in between. You can view his photos at www.facebook.com/jhofmannphoto.

ACKNOWLEDGMENTS

Thanks to Mom and Dad for never really minding what color hair I came home with and William Joseph Jolly for saving my strands, getting them healthy, and keeping me red for most of my twenties. You're my favorite!

Many thanks to the models who donated their time and hairdos to make this book: Laura Levey, Alisson Furman, Ashley Prine, Kathryn Welles, Lana Rose Diaz, and Agnieszka (Aggie) Wszolkowska.

CPSIA information can be obtained
at www.ICGtesting.com
Printed in the USA
LVHW011130261021
701521LV00001B/3

9 781646 042647